SQUIT AND WIT
WITH KNOBS ON!

Keith Skipper

MP

SQUIT and WIT
with KNOBS ON!

Published in 2013

by:

Mousehold Press
Victoria Cottage
Constitution Opening
Norwich NR3 4BD
www.mousehold-press.co.uk

ISBN 978-1-874739-68-5

printed by Mimeo, Huntingdon

ACKNOWLEDGEMENTS

I am grateful to Radio Norfolk for allowing certain features of its more cultural output to be included here in printed form. It goes to show you can sometimes be led to believe what you hear.

David Clayton's uplifting foreword underlines the spirit in which our local radio station has embraced the need for some squit to go with all the BBC polish.

Publisher Adrian Bell again pins our gloriously parochial colours to the mast – or perhaps that should be transmitter – with his customary good humour and unflappable support.

Special thanks to Stewart Orr for the loan of one of his vintage wireless sets to adorn the cover, to Paul Damen and others who provided photographs and to Richard Shepheard and Ivan Lilley for leading the parade of guest story-tellers.

To all my fellow–panellists and Should The Team Think? backing crews over the years – including so many enthusiastic audiences – I dedicate this little slice of home-made fun as a shining example of what care in the community really means.

Making each other laugh is free and priceless.

To make this here programme a hit
Take some people of wisdom and wit
Stir in some direction
Half-bake to perfection
And you'll end up with this load of old squit

FOREWORD

By David Clayton – Editor of BBC Radio Norfolk and Chairman of Should The Team Think?

I've been quoted as saying that Should The Team Think? is about as much fun as grown men can have with their clothes on.

I know that's a frightening image but a whimsical radio panel game, invented in a pub, has kept Skip and I enjoying too much proper, fully-clothed fun for over a couple of decades.

Should The Team Think? was a dare between us back in the early 1990s. Could we do a Norfolk-style radio panel game? How would it sound? What would be in it?

We thought one might work...but did we have the courage to give it a go? The answer to all those questions was a resounding "YES!". We've taken the panel game (and the radio recording of it) all over Norfolk to joyous receptions of mirth and laughter. Then the recordings have played out on BBC Radio Norfolk. Cue county-wide hilarity!

Skip and I are rather proud our "dare" is still rumbling on, albeit occasionally and each time in the name of some Norfolk charity. Much of the whimsy has come off the cuff but inevitably some of it needs writing down. There's none better than Keith Skipper MBE to author it and then file it away for Norfolk posterity.

In truth the man has been treading the boards in all sorts of guises over the years, dishing out a humorous line in the name of his beloved Norfolk. He's accumulated a treasure trove of wit and squit. It was inevitable a book from Norfolk's most prolific author would gather it all together.

As chairman of Should The Team Think? I've probably managed only a loose hand on the tiller, so to speak. Some argue I regularly lose control of the panellists. But when you're in the company of Keith Skipper you know he's in possession of a bottomless pit of ideas and anecdotes to produce another blast of laughter from the audience. When he wasn't, there was always Sid Kipper and a famous cast to pop in a punchline.

So enjoy this miscellany of mirth, this lexicon of laughter, this gaggle of giggles. It comes tried and tested in front of that most discerning of audiences – YOU!

INTRODUCTION

If the best pictures are still on the wireless, it should follow that some of the biggest and best laughs should keep on floating over the airwaves.

For those of us weaned on the glories of radio comedy – and I wrote my 11-plus exam essay in 1955 on why I loved Educating Archie – it comes as no surprise to find such a cheerful following for a homely tribute programme nodding so appreciatively towards a whole series of family favourites.

BBC Radio Norfolk's Should The Team Think? is the main inspiration behind this towering volume, vibrant and visionary without ever veering towards the vitriolic or vituperative. A travelling show dispensing dazzling wit and whimsy since 1993 surely deserves such a permanent accolade in print.

It was a cause of immense satisfaction for me when this much-loved panel game was staged before a full house in the Pavilion Theatre at the end of Cromer Pier in October, 2012, to mark my proud half-century as a Norfolk mardler and scribe. Special guest the Bishop of Norwich, the Rt. Rev. Graham James, brought an overdue air of respectability to proceedings, a blessing from which the show could find it hard to recover.

I can remember chuckling along with Does The Team Think? (nearly as good a title as the Norfolk version) on the old Light Programme as Jimmy Edwards, Arthur Askey, Ted Ray and a guest panellist each week played questions and answers for laughs while the suave McDonald Hobley tried to keep order.

It was a heart-warming parody of Any Questions? in which serious issues of the hour were debated by important people like politicians, writers and personalities with axes to grind ... if only David Dimbleby had thought of pinching that idea for television!

While silly panel games packed with so-called celebrities litter current television schedules, it must be significant that I'm Sorry I Haven't A Clue on Radio 4 continues to attract and hold multitudes of discerning listeners of all ages despite the loss of long-serving chairman, the wonderfully enigmatic Humphrey Lytttleton.

Fishing line – Starfish and Huss

A notable jazzman, he was surprise choice in 1972 to host this 'antidote to all panel games'. His disgruntled, deadpan and occasionally utterly bewildered style of chairmanship added extra layers of comedy, a straight man surrounded by mayhem but always ready to risk the most outrageous *double entendre.*

It was as if The Goon Show and Round the Horne had found a way down Mornington Crescent to inject a bit of daring and dash into Humph's deliberations. Oh, for a quick burst of Bluebottle Blues or the tender strains of the Song of the Bogle Clencher by Rambling Syd Rumpo.

Mind you, several episodes of Should The Team Think? recorded in front of shamelessly live audiences across the county had to embrace off-the-wall ponderings and under-the-radar observations of a rambling Sid Kipper. In the end, he convinced us all we were better for it.

The sage of St Just-near-Trunch has graciously agreed to adorn the following pages with a smattering of his wit-and-wisdom talents, some first on show in cultural fleshpots such as Foulsham and Frettenham and others in the illuminating columns of the *Merry Mawkin*, a regular publication espousing the joyful views of Friends Of Norfolk Dialect.

Sid also created furiously in the name of tantalising limericks to coax fellow panellists into occasionally dodgy waters in response to the chairman's challenge at the start of each instalment. I have added a host more from a collection garnered over the amusing years.

Call Me an Old Bluffer became a cheerful cornerstone of the show as members of the audience were thrust into the spotlight at random to work out which smooth operator on stage was telling the truth. Plenty of chances to spot a drop of honesty in a sea of subterfuge as these pages unfold.

Other examples of uplifting off-the-cuff squit like late arrivals for various balls and excruciating fishing lines share remaining honours with favourite yarns, poems, pictorial teasers and a few light-hearted articles from my *Eastern Daily Press* output.

Readers played a key part in my plans for a big finish to this celebratory tome with their contributions to A Sort of Norfolk Dictionary starring alternate meanings for well-known words and

Fishing line – Codfinger

phrases. Did this bright idea also feature on another BBC radio panel game? I'm sorry but I haven't a clue.

It's nearly as much fun reflecting on Should The Team Think? adventures as it could be taking part in them. There may be more to come if that old adage about fooling all the people all of the time stands true and pure squit continues as one of Norfolk's most precious commodities.

In any event, I warmly salute my fellow-panellists, unflappable producer Tony Mallion and engineering crews who must have wondered why all outside broadcasts couldn't be like this.

A special nod of appreciation for chairman David Clayton, who must take at least half of the blame for an outstanding radio success threatening to translate into Norfolk folklore.

And a lingering sense of deep gratitude for all who have attended shows, tuned into them for more cultural refreshment … and now bought this book to prove it wasn't just a dream.

Keith Skipper,
Cromer, 2013

Skip, Sid and Henry Blogg

CALL ME AN OLD BLUFFER

One of the most popular features of BBC Radio Norfolk's legendary panel game, Should The Team Think?, saw an unsuspecting member of the audience invited to work out who might be telling the truth on stage.

I came up with the idea of this light-hearted guessing interlude to allow panellists opportunities to reveal unlikely dramatic qualities as they took on various guises or tried to convince the listener that their interpretation of an old word or time-honoured custom was indeed the authentic one.

Call Me an Old Bluffer soon became an integral part of cultural proceedings as the travelling show built up a lengthy list of appreciative locations. Special guests, including the Bishop of Norwich, the Rt. Rev. Graham James, joined in the teasing fun and it was rare for that randomly chosen member of the audience to come up with the right answer at the first go.

This volume features a few rounds from the programme's colourful history starring ancient dialect words, old-fashioned remedies, quaint traditions and outstanding characters from all walks of life. Only one out of each quartet is true … and even those who attended the shows or tuned in to the recordings will be hard pushed to recall many, if any, honest presentations such was the sincerity with which all were delivered.

So size up the offerings dotted among the following pages, blow away the bluffing froth and reveal the glorious truth. Answers at back of the book (page 81). If you get them all correct, don't rest on your laurels. Make up your own version and test out family and friends.

Fishing line – Look Stickleback in Anger

Mystery guest, BBC Television's David Whiteley, fourth along, joins the panel for a chat after his identity has been revealed at the Pavilion Theatre on Cromer Pier in October, 2012. This show marked Keith Skipper's 50th year as Norfolk mardler and scribe.

Fishing line – Moll Flounders

CALL ME AN OLD BLUFFER - 1
SPOT THE REAL OLD LOCAL REMEDY

Cowpat capers – A North Norfolk fisherman went into a pub with his right hand heavily bandaged. He explained that while gutting a fish he got a bone buried into his hand and had been unable to remove it. The pub landlord immediately sent one of his customers into a nearby field to fetch a large dock leaf and a cowpat. The fresh cow manure was placed on the man's hand which was then wrapped around with the dock leaf. Half an hour later the poultice was removed and there was the white end of the cod bone sticking up. It was easily removed. There followed a great celebration in the pub – and the man who had benefited put his restored hand in his pocket and bought a round. Pick the bones out of that one!

Troubles behind – A traditional cure for piles in the west of the county involved a rocking horse with its reins trimmed with laurel leaves and, for those who wanted to go all the way, a nosebag containing crushed gooseberries. The human sufferer was bid to mount the horse carefully and rock it no less than 36 times while reciting the lines:

> Horsey, horsey, please be kind
> And leave my troubles all behind
> Horsey, horsey, bring me smiles
> And take away these painful piles!

It is claimed the remedy worked best when the rider was dressed in a military uniform. That's a traditional cure for piles from the west of Norfolk, in use up to the late 1890s.

Whooping it up – There are many traditional remedies for whooping cough, such as consumption of roasted mouse – crisply done on both sides. But one of the lesser-known cures for what was once a very common ailment among youngsters involved an acorn ground into pulp and then mixed with rainwater from a wooden tub or wooden vessel. It had to be wooden. The mixture was not consumed in any way but applied gently to the outside of the throat while the nose and ears were pinched quite sharply. This was supposed to squeeze the cough out while the mixture of acorn pulp and water protected the throat from further infection. If an acorn could not be found it was permissible to use dried peas.

A healthy dip – This is a tried and trusted remedy for hiccups particularly popular among Norfolk farmworkers at the end of the 1800s. Hiccups were a common complaint among these labourers who often ate far too quickly or talked while trying to drink out of a bottle. The proven cure was for the worker to be dipped into the nearest pond or running stream, making sure the left ear was fully immersed. This was then wiped immediately on a chaff sack used specifically for that purpose. The old 'ear-rubber' was standard material on most farms. Immersion of the ear evidently restored proper balance to the senses – and the hiccups would possibly stop within seconds. It was the sack's special remedial properties that made sure it worked.

"Welcome to another extravaganza of Norfolk fun and games!" –
Should The Team Think? chairman David Clayton in expansive mood.

Fishing line - The Clambusters

LATE ARRIVALS ...
... FOR THE HORTICULTURAL BALL

Please welcome Mr and Mrs Bacious-Border and their elder son Herb Bacious-Border

A warm reception if you would be so kind for the Rhynum family... Mr and Mrs Rhynum, the little Rhynums (nursery Rhynums), Uncle Rhynum and the belle of the ball, Auntie Rhynum.

We are delighted to welcome Mr and Mrs Postheap and their Irish cousin, Com Postheap

Not forgetting Mr and Mrs Clippings-Pyle and their son, country and western singer Lorne Clippings-Pyle.

Please be upstanding for Lord Bird, Lady Bird and their little Bishy-Barney-Bees.

Here's the Queen of the Onion Patch – the Lady of Shallott.

And the singing sensation, Miss Petunia Clark.

And finally, please welcome illustrious members of the Seed family. First, the twins, Ani Seed and Poppy Seed, their Italian cousin Inter Seed, black sheep of the family Con Seed, top policeman Super Seed, rather deaf Uncle Hey? Seed, and the latest arrival, the pretty baby known as Suck Seed.

In all, they're worth a packet.

"Wonder who it can be ... ". Keith Skipper and special panellist the Bishop of Norwich, the Rt Rev Graham James, are kept in the dark on stage at Cromer.

Fishing line – Eel Met by Moonlight

MARRIAGE LINES

The local radio station was interviewing an 80-year-old woman because she had just married for the fourth time. The interviewer asked her questions about her life, about what it felt like to be marrying again at 80, and then about her new husband's occupation.

"He's a funeral director," she answered.

"Interesting," the newsman thought.

He then asked her if she wouldn't mind telling him a little about her first three husbands and what they did for a living.

She paused for a few moments, needing time to reflect on all those years. After a short time a smile came to her face and she answered proudly, explaining that she had first married a banker when she was in her early 20s. Then a circus ringmaster when in her 40s. Then a preacher when in her 60s and now in her 80s the funeral director.

The interviewer looked at her, quite astonished, and asked why she had married four men with such diverse careers.

She smiled and patiently explained:

"I married one for the money, two for the show, three to get ready, and four to go."

When they asked me to write on manure
My ideas could not have be fewer
Nevertheless
I think this should impress
The EDP's poetry reviewer

Fishing line – Whiting for Codot

17

NORFOLK FIRSTS: *Norfolk's first official lottery draw was organised by Florrie Flutter in the back kitchen of her Winfarthing cottage. There were full houses for three months in 1922 as ticket buyers queued to guess her age. Interest waned when it was rumoured she was an actress of 25 masquerading as an old maid. She moved to a bungalow in Quidenham on the proceeds.*

Fishing Line – Catch 22

LONG LIVE SQUIT

I'm often asked for my favourite Norfolk yarns and reasons why they have lasted so long.

See, an automatic assumption that I am ancient while our highly individual sense of humour, a potent mixture of squit, wit and shifty tales doused in dialect, is little more than an affectionate nod towards a gentler, slower age.

Perhaps the disappearance of so many good ole boys from cosy corners of our local pubs and a dramatic decline in numbers working on the land have cut off vital fresh supplies of earthy fun to the Norfolk Laughter Grid.

No doubt a grubby tide of stand-up spite and confrontational capers masquerading as entertainment has washed away most grounds for belief in a television service bent on provoking healthy laughter.

Comedian Vic Reeves, clearly pining for the good old days of Morecambe and Wise, Tommy Cooper, The Two Ronnies and Les Dawson, lamented recently: "Comedy has become very bitter. It's got quite nasty, quite venomous." Some will suggest he could have left "quite" out of that timely little script.

It's all very well claiming our comedy has to reflect hard times, question entrenched attitudes and force us to face up to difficult truths. But that begs no excuse for embarrassingly large rations of cruelty and crudeness, not even towards greedy bankers, blinkered politicians and football managers who must know their stupid or inflammatory words will be taken as gospel by so many.

Humour employed properly can diffuse messy situations, cut through cant and hypocrisy and throw a gentle light on scary dark corners. Humour ought to make us smile and think, not wince, worry and rant.

Wholesome Norfolk squit, with its stunning use of understatement, may have its roots in days when folk had to provide their own amusement or go without. Even so, I sense it could yet play an important role in our emergence from economic and spiritual depression.

From whence springs such new-dawn optimism? Well, I have witnessed enough revivals built on old-fashioned virtues and homely chuckles to appreciate anew sentiments expressed by rural writer Clarence Henry Warren about 70 years ago.

He mused: "It is one of the most attractive features of country humour that it never quite loses its freshness. It may be passed on from generation to generation but it remains a coin whose mintage is never dulled with use.

"The same may be said of country expressions which are not necessarily humorous at all – metaphors and likenesses and odd phrases which, once coined, have never gone out of currency."

He recalled a couple of his father's sayings: "It doesn't take long to do a five-minute job." And to anyone out and about unusually early in the morning: "You must have got up before you went anywhere."

Old boys in my home village would have added how often it picks a wet day to rain, how it gets late earlier when the clocks go back and how often they knocked a hole in the wall so they could dip their bread in next door's gravy.

I'm still collecting nuggets on my Norfolk rounds, more like little pebbles of whimsy dropped into oceans of debate about incinerators, wind turbines, council cuts, car parking charges and people who move to Norfolk and can only see a joke by appointment.

There's the one about Charlie showing a party of tourists round Great Yarmouth. He pointed out the very spot where Lord Nelson supposedly threw a gold sovereign across the River Yare. "That is impossible," snapped one of the visitors. "No-one could throw coins that distance."

"Ah, but yew hev ter remember," explained Charlie, "money went a rare lot farther in them days."

This one reached me via a regular source of material pounding the mean streets of Cromer. It features two venerable local characters watching a hearse rolling slowly by. As it disappeared into the distance, one inquired: "Who died, then?"

"Him in the box, I reckon" said the other.

"Yis," pondered the first, "driver looked orryte."

A Norfolk vicar dropped this on my collection plate. During his talk to the children, the young curate asked, "What is grey, has a bushy tail and gathers nuts in the autumn?"

Little Horry at the back raised his hand. "I know th'arnser orter be Jesus – but that dew sound wholly like a squirrel ter me."

Right, as you've read this far, I offer as a reward a couple from my Top 10. The others are on the way to BBC Television's Head of Light Entertainment.

Martha's husband died and she went to put an announcement in the local paper. She wanted to keep it as short as possible. "Jist put 'Billy Grimble dead'." She suggested. The girl told her she could have six words for the same price.

"Right," said Martha. "Kin yew add 'Ferret for sale.'"

Finally, Jacob and Eliza were relaxing in front of the fire as anniversary cards trembled on the mantelpiece above. The old gal turned to her husband of 70 years and asked: "Bor, if I should go afore yew, will yew promise me if yew tearke on sumwun else yew wunt let har wear my clothes?"

"Dunt yew fret, my bewty, cors I wunt" replied Jacob.

"Ennyway, they wunt fit."

Eastern Daily Press, February, 2012

WIT AND WISDOM OF SID KIPPER

A rare Norfolk word; Coypu

Now at one time of the day people in Norfolk talked of little else but coypu, but if you was to ask a young Norfolk man or mawther what a coypu was now, they'd more than likely tell you it was what a sneaky cow done in the corner of a field. Well, what do they know?

Some years ago coypu rampaged across the county, devouring children and terrifying old ladies. They especially liked the Broads, which people used to think was very old. Of course, now we know the Broads was dug out by a bloke called Pete, and got filled with water in a heavy downpour.

The coypu liked to live in banks, which was all right until you wanted to get your money out. Because then you might find they'd chewed it all up.

Obviously when they affected people with money that couldn't be allowed to go on, so the Coypu Control was invented. Well, actually it already existed but up till then it had only been there to stop the coypu getting drunk and causing disturbances in Ranworth, due to the people of Ranworth being quite capable of causing their own disturbances.

But now the job was to catch the coypu, confirm they was illegal immigrants and then send them back where they come from. Only no one was quite sure where that was, so a lot of them got eaten.

If you must know they were a bit like rabbit, but less hoppy.

After a bit there was no more coypu in Norfolk, so people stopped talking about them, because obviously people weren't interested in anything not in Norfolk. Except London, of course, but people only talk about that to moan about it.

And so you got to where we are today which is no coypu, but a lot of Londoners.

And they call that progress.

CALL ME AN OLD BLUFFER - 2
WHAT'S THE REAL MEANING OF OLD WORD 'LAGARAG'?

Nasty nits – Lagarag was a common name used in many parts of Norfolk to describe nits in the hair. It was heard regularly in schools when the nit nurse came round to inspect. "She'll sort him out – he's got lagarag." It is thought to have been derived from an Indian word brought back to Norfolk by soldiers who had served in that country. There is an old Hindu word for fleas that sounds like it.

Class party – This was the name given to an end-of-term party at some posher schools in this area at the end of the 19th century. It was mentioned in classic literature by no less an author than Charles Dickens in David Copperfield when Steerforth and Co celebrated the end of term with a wild lagarag. It culminated in three pupils being expelled for inviting three young ladies of easy virtue into their dormitory late at night. Pleased to report that young Copperfield was not one of the offenders.

Lazy streak – This word is rather suitable for a Should The Team Think? panel as it describes a lazy sort who will do no more work than necessary to get by. In fact, the person in question needs constant prodding to do anything. It was once in regular usage in both Norfolk and Suffolk. There's an obvious association between a lazy person and someone finishing up in no more than rags. A perfect summary for certain employees, both past and present, of the BBC!

Spot the hanky – Lagarag is an old Norfolk colloquialism for the spotted handkerchief in which released prisoners tied up all their meagre possessions before marching off down the road to respectability. It makes good sense – old lag, common parlance for someone used to doing time, and a rag to describe he material in which their bits and pieces were tied up. It was used liberally until the 1930s. Then like many other expressions, it disappeared after the war.

Fishing line – Some Pike it Hot (with Jack Lemon-Sole)

DAZZLING WORDPLAY

They've been round the block a few times but there are certain examples of dazzling wordplay designed to cheer up those of us depressed by abominations like "gutted" and "gobsmacked" and other lurid examples of trendybabble.

I remember with joy a sales pitch in the window of a local camping and leisure shop. It read: "Now is the winter of our discount tent." Friends spotted an optician's sign suggesting "If you don't see what you want, you've come to the right place" and a sad little note in the door of a closed-down bookshop informing the world – "Words failed us."

Graffiti gems collected over the years include "Alas, poor Yorlik, I knew him backwards", "Down with categorical imperatives!", "The day after tomorrow is the third day of the rest of your life" and "Spell-checks are hear two stay."

Perhaps the best riposte of recent times complete with distinctive Norfolk flavour came from the old boy who was asked if he knew what jargon was. "Jargon?" he echoed. "Cors I know what jargon is. Thass what hully fit local people dew afore breakfast – they go a 'jargon!"

A useful starting point for another look at what is happening to our beautiful language. How much more gobbledegook, bureaucratese, doublespeak, jargon and unadulterated rubbish must we endure before the next party political conference season?

It is too easy to blame the Americans for all this linguistic squit as they work overtime to take nastiness out of brutal reality by offering "energetic disassembly" for a nuclear power plant explosion, "uncontrolled contact with the ground" for an aircraft crash and "unlawful or arbitrary deprivation of life" for killing. We must own up to several long-winded stinkers of our own. Slums and ghettos have given way to inner cities and sub-standard housing. You know, where the fiscal under-achievers hang out wondering where the next quantitive easing might be coming from while ignoring the values of nutritional avoidance therapy.

The art of making 50 words do the job of two has reached epidemic levels. It all points to spreading confusion, to drive a wedge between

Fishing line – David Kipperfield

24

what is said or written and what is meant. I repeat we ought to put our own house in order before casting stones at others. Like the White House who told us a few years back that President Reagan wasn't really unconscious when he underwent surgery – just in "a non-decision-making form."

Every trade or profession has its own jargon. For example, lawyers, accountants and estate agents are okay while they're chatting to like-minded colleagues, but how can they be expected to communicate with ordinary mortals?

Broadcasters and journalists are just as awkwardly placed. I know from experience how the BBC is riddled with initials and obsessed with sending round memos containing a few hundred of them at a time. They can even flummox those they are supposed to enlighten.

I realised in time that HOB stood for Head Of Broadcasting but I won few friends in high places for suggesting regular audiences with him could be construed as Hobnobbing.

In my broadcasting years, radio presenters presumed listeners knew what they meant by prefade, sting, cart, segue. Newspaper reporters still lose themselves in intros, paras, nibs, mag cts and cncl mtgs.

Football spokesmen – and how they have proliferated since I was a lad in long shorts – wallow in a mixture of the amusingly banal and the utterly pointless. Managers love to be patronised, responding with quality quotes like "If we stick to the basics and remember our good habits we should get a result." They mean a win, draw or defeat – so there can be no arguing with that kind of prognostication.

It does seem talk is cheap on most sporting fronts. I can't wait for priceless interviews from the Olympics before and after the event.

"How do you rate your chances?"

"I'll tell you when it's over."

"When did you feel you had gold in your grasp?"

"When I won."

Now, a chat with someone who finishes a surprising last in his heat would make a pleasant change...

"Look here, you were supposed to wipe the floor with this lot. How come you made such a pig's ear out of it and trailed behind opponents who'd never been on a track before?"

"Well, Brendan, you see, we had a bit of a party in my chalet last night and it's hard to see the hurdles let alone clear them when you have a stinking hangover."

During my early days as a newspaper reporter, just as custodians and pivots were disappearing from our soccer pitches, I found committee meeting minutes hard to follow. Experienced colleagues offered sound advice such as converting the "proposed erection of 24 superior dwellings" into plans for two dozen new homes.

Keep it simple. No point in thrusting a notebook under the nose of a celebrating centenarian and inquiring: "To what do you owe your longevity?" Or asking a Little Dunham farmer: "How are your grain-consuming animal units coming on, ole partner?"

So, at this moment in time after a full and frank exchange of views across the board, I await the signal from more sensitive and clear-minded folk that they are going off jargon.
The exercise will do them good.

Eastern Daily Press – May, 2012

HOLY WATER

Did you hear about the Bishop of Norwich who went fishing?

He was spending a pleasant day out with friends in a boat on a lake in the heart of Norfolk.

He suddenly realised he'd left his packed lunch on the bank. She got out of the boat, walked across the water and collected his sandwiches. Then he walked back to the boat.

Next day a big headline in the *Eastern Daily Press* read:

BISHOP OF NORWICH
CANNOT SWIM!

Fishing line – Porgy and Bass

UNWRAP THE REAL CHRISTMAS CUSTOM

Marathon bells–When Christmas Day fell on a Friday it was customary in the town of East Dereham to ring the parish church bells non-stop for five hours from first light. The peals would be muffled in the early stages. We know about this tradition from the famous diary of Benjamin Armstrong, who was vicar here in Victorian times. For example, he wrote in December, 1873: "They will ring briefly on the morrow for the stoning of St Stephen. Such a marathon on this blessed Friday is for the deafening of all within range of St Nicholas!" The tradition ended in the 1890s when Armstrong's successor organised a petition after countless complaints.

Boxing Day fish – Courting couples in and around Great Yarmouth had good reason to look forward to Boxing Day in the late 1800s and early years of the following century. It was customary for a dozen loving partnerships to be summoned to the town hall after the drawing of lots to receive a cran of fresh herring to bless their relationship. If they happened to wed before the next Boxing Day they would be invited back, without taking part in a lottery, to be awarded a salting of sprats, thought to possess significant qualities in the name of fertility. Many years later there was a touching reunion at the Wrestler's Inn pub near the market place when 27 couples who collected both herring and sprats celebrated their Boxing Day bonanza.

Wassailing warrior – It was once a colourful tradition of many villages in the north of Norfolk to elect a chief "wassailing warrior" to carry the lantern at the head of carol-singing parties around the vicinity. Although it was not obligatory, the honour usually went to the vicar or curate on the assumption that the presence of such an important local figure would loosen purse strings at the door. The chief wassailing warrior had the right to choose the first carol to be sung at the parish church carol service.

Maiden's watch – Maidens of all ages and all kinds anxious to find a husband would keep special watch on Christmas Eve. The idea was that she who waited for a glimpse of her future spouse would wash out her chemise – that's a seductive one-piece undergarment, usually a loose, straight-hanging dress – placing it before the fire to dry. The expectant maiden would then wait in solemn silence until midnight when her chosen one would come in and turn the linen. This was a true sign of festive romance – maidens watching and waiting for Romeo to appear.

NORFOLK FIRSTS: *Norfolk's only known professional snake charmer was Bolshie Billhooks, a former bed salesman from Little Snoring. He gave popular demonstrations of his art on Litcham Common where his patter featured the immortal line: "I defy mathematics to take away your adders." His autobiography, A Load of Old Cobras, was a modest success.*

DENVER SINGALONG

Stetson Electic Country & Western was the name of an American group touring the world to give their renditions of various famous pieces in the style of the original artists.

Their vow was always the same: if a number was called and they could not duplicate it, they would forfeit a thousand dollars, or equivalent, to the person who had named the song.

There was one condition. The person concerned had to sing a few bars of the number.

They had a barnstorming tour in the United Kingdom and no-one had called their bluff. Then they reached Norfolk to meet a huge gathering of Country & Western fans at a great barn in the Fens.

The night was going swimmingly with renditions of winners by Dolly Parton, Glen Campbell, Willie Nelson, Don Williams and many others. Percy, an aged Norfolk rustic, then got up and asked for "Farmer Jack".

This threw the group into turmoil. They went into a huddle and then the lead singer confessed. They were stymied by Percy's request and would be only too pleased to cough up £500 if he met with their condition of a personal shot at the opening of the ballad.

Percy jumps forward and grabs the mike. Then in the tones of Denver (Sluice, not Colorado), he crooned:

> Farmer Jack to a king
> From loneliness to a wedding ring
> I played an ace and I won a queen
> And walked away with your heart

EYE SPY

Once in an old Norfolk village, they say
Lived a maiden quite shapely and wise
She was nearly so normal in every way
But sadly, this girl had THREE eyes

Some of the local lads giggled and mocked
As she smiled at them from the veranda
They sang, I, I, I, but she never seemed shocked
So they nick-named her Carmen Miranda

When she rode on her cycle, her eyes were a sight
As off through the roadways she sped
With one looking left, one looking right
And one looking dead-straight ahead

On shopping day, after she'd finished her calls
To relax her three eyes, she would stop
And focus her gaze on the three big brass balls
Hanging over the pawnbrokers' shop

One day, this poor three-eyed girl lost her heart
To a one-eyed Peruvian spy
But after a while, they decided to part
Cos they just couldn't see eye to eye

But so sad to say, a car got in the way
As she staggered one night, from the local
So please spare a thought for that lass, far away
And be thankful you're only bi-focal

IMPORTANCE OF WALKING

Walking can add minutes to your life. This enables you at 85 years old to spend an additional five months in a nursing home at £700 per month.

My grandpa started walking five miles a day when he was 60. Now he's 97 years old and we don't know where the hell he is.

I like long walks, especially when they are taken by people who annoy me.

The only reason I would take up walking is so that I could hear heavy breathing again.

I have to walk early in the morning, before my brain figures out what I'm doing.

I joined a health club last year, spent about £400. Haven't lost a pound. Apparently you have to go there.

I do have flabby thighs, but fortunately my stomach covers them.

The advantage of exercising every day is so when you die, they'll say: "Well, he looks good, doesn't he?"

If you are going to try cross-country ski-ing, start with a small country.

I know I got a lot of exercise the last few years – just getting over the hill.

An adventurer hailing from Loddon
Liked to go where none ever had troddon
So he walked on the Broads
And crossed rivers by fords
Coming back with his plimsolls quite soddon

CALL ME AN OLD BLUFFER - 4
WHAT'S THE TRUE MEANING OF OLD WORD 'DAFTER'?

Class act – This was a special dialect word used by many schoolteachers in Norfolk, especially in the villages, to describe a dunce. They didn't want to use the word "dunce" and so they invented one they thought marginally less demeaning. "He's a right dafter ... might as well go bird-scaring" was the sort of comment reserved for pupils who found it impossible to keep up with the rest.

Comic turn – This was the rather clever name given to the most prominent member of a comedy double act doing the rounds in Norfolk and Suffolk village halls before the second world war. It meant quite simply that one was dafter than the other – and so the one leading the way on stage was afforded that label. That's dafter – the rustic Morecambe to the rustic Wise.

Early scarecrow – Dafter was a fore-runner of the mawkin. Rather outlandish scarecrows wearing bright coloured garments were called dafters in some parts of Norfolk and Suffolk until the early part of the 20th century. The obvious insinuation was that birds had to be daft to be scared off by such comical looking creatures.

Girl talk – the word simply means daughter, just following the pronunciation of a word like "laughter." There is a record in a certain Norfolk parish from the 18th century that shows all female children baptised in a 20-year period were entered on the register as "dafters." It may just be playing around with sounds and words but it makes good sense. Dafter – a daughter.

There was a comedian from Gt Ellingham
Who was booked to perform at the millennium
But his jokes they fell flat
And the reason for that
It was simply the way he was tellinum

A thoughtful Sid Kipper teams up with Karen Buchanan on stage at Stalham

Mawther Maggie, a Radio Norfolk favourite for many years, warms up the audience with some of her home-made whimsy before another show unfolds in the name of high culture.

NORFOLK FIRSTS: *Norfolk's earliest dating agency "for the shy and retiring" was set up at Spooner Row in 1907. Here are the first couple to meet on the famous "bashful bench" at sunset, Ophelia Green from Scarning and Ernest Balls from North Elmham. They heeded parental advice and did not marry.*

Fishing line – The Blue Lamprey

WIT AND WISDOM OF SID KIPPER
Dot Kipper's recipes

These recipes come from my old mother's book, *Dot Kipper's Handy Household Hints*. I've got a rare first edition. Mind you, that's not as rare as a second edition would be.

Dressed Crab – This is an old Victorian recipe, due to the fact that they were shocked by nude crabs.

Ingredients: One crab (or another); knitting wool; needles.

Method: Cook the crab in the normal way, and allow to cool. Meanwhile knit it a jumper, remembering to give it eight arms and no neck. When the crab is cool, and you're hot and bothered, dress it with the jumper'

Tip: Never try to dress a live crab, as it won't thank you for it and will probably only nip you for your troubles, but that won't cure them – you need bees for that.

(At one time crabs were kept as pets in North Norfolk. The practice died out due to their lack of affection and the fact that when they were placed in the sort of exercise wheel used for hamsters they simply walked out sideways.)

Been Sprouts – The name of this recipe comes from the answer to the question: "What's this?"

Ingredients; Sprouts (one per person is quite enough).

Method: Boil the sprouts in salted water for a few hours, until they go a nasty colour and break up. Serve with chicken, pork, or anything else to take the taste away.

Tip: The recipe is best served for guests who have overstayed their welcome or never had one in the first place. Other things that have the same effect is Damp Squid, Bumpkin Pie and Sour Grapes.

 (The habit of using food as a heavy hint seems to have been universal. In Lincolnshire, they would serve Fritters, so called because people were frightened to eat them. And few people have ever attempted a second London Derriere.)

IT'S A FAIR COP

A Norfolk man was on his way to bed one night when his wife told him he'd left the light on in the shed. She could see the light from their bedroom window.

The man took a look for himself and saw there were burglars in the shed taking things.

He phoned the police who said no-one was available to help at that time but they would send someone over as soon as they were available.

He replied "Okay", hung up and waited a minute. Then he phoned the police back and said: "I called you just a minute ago to tell you about burglars in my shed. Well, you don't have to worry about them now. I've just shot 'em."

Within five minutes there were half a dozen police cars on the scene, an armed response unit, and the full works. Of course, they caught the burglars red-handed.

One of the officers remarked: "Thought you said you'd shot 'em"

The man replied: "I thought you said there was nobody available."

> There was an old Bishop of Lynn
> Who preached that to murder is sin,
> But each evening at seven
> This servant of Heaven
> Sat down and he murdered a gin.

Fishing line – Tunas of Glory

LATE ARRIVALS ...
...FOR THE FARMERS' BALL

Ladies and gentlemen, please welcome your president and his wife, Mr and Mrs Sutra, along with their agricultural student son with romantic notions, young Farmer Sutra.

Your attention please for Mr and Mrs Orpington and their modelling daughter, Buff Orpington.

A warm welcome to our special visitors from afar – Scottish farmer, Angus McSpreader, Welsh hill farmer, Dai Versify, and Dublin farmer, Paddy Fields with his faithful dog, Irish Setterside.

And here we have local personalities Mr and Mrs Fencing and their son Rick. He's standing as a candidate in the forthcoming NFU elections... hence the current popular slogan "Elect Rick Fencing!"

And finally, please welcome our main guests for this auspicious occasion, Mr and Mrs Fishal Insemination and their frisky son ... Artie Fishal Insemination.

Early members of the Norfolk Flat Earth Society
on their way to a meeting in Sloley

I paid my debts – I'm Drifter Parkes from Stiffkey on the north Norfolk coast. I was transported to Australia in 1841 for stealing sheep, turnips and chickens from a farm at Morston nearby. I was known as Drifter as I took casual labour on a number of farms and smallholdings in the area for ridiculously low wages. It was impossible to feed and clothe my family of 13 and that's why I resorted to helping myself. Ironically, I became a very successful sheep farmer in northern Queensland and returned to Stiffkey in 1874. One of the first things I did was to go back to Stonepit Farm from where I had stolen sheep, turnips and chickens to pay the owner, who was still there, full remuneration

Beer with a kick – I'm Joshua Grimwade of Catfield, not far from Stalham. I was sentenced to death in 1823 for poisoning my next door neighbour Abel Smart. He made home-made beer, gallons of the stuff, but was very reluctant to share any with either family or friends. Although I say it myself, I did many favours for my neighbour, who was slightly disabled after an accident on the farm, but not once did he show a grain of gratitude. So, in March 1823, I took some rat poison next door and tipped it into one of his casks in the back room. The police were called three weeks later when he was found dead beside the beer.... pointing to my window next door. I broke down eventually under questioning and met my end in Norwich in November that year.

Arsenic and old dumplings – I'm Fanny Alexander of Wretton, a mile from Stoke Ferry and six miles from Downham. I was acquitted in 1842 of attempting to murder my husband by putting arsenic in his dumplings. As if I would! I told the police the powder must have fallen from the shelf above while I was making them. My dear husband Terrington ate three and I ate one. We were both very sick and I would hardly poison myself. There were silly claims that I was trying to get rid of my husband because I was seeing another man. Quite rightly, the judge directed the jury to acquit me as there simply wasn't enough evidence to show I deliberately put the arsenic in the dumplings. He did warn about leaving fatal poisons carelessly around the house and told me to go home and be faithful and good to my husband.

Chapter of accidents – I'm Noel Gallant, better known as the Dereham Dandy. In the early 1800s I gave up a possible career in law to pursue a more colourful and lucrative course, wooing and charming elderly ladies of considerable means. Once they had pledged part of their fortune to me – most were rich widows of the town – they happened to meet unfortunately fatal accidents. Mary Millington fell off her horse because the saddle was insecure. Hannah Lark walked into a pond when her lantern failed. Grace Hapgood was fatally wounded by a wild pig which suddenly appeared at our picnic near Gressenhall. My career ended in 1837 when Martha Spinks, a feisty 79-year-old, awoke to give the alarm as I tried to smother her with a pillow. I was found guilty of multiple murders at Norfolk Assizes and hanged at the Castle in 1838.

NORFOLK FIRSTS: *Norfolk's first district nurse Ethel Nightingale (no relation to Lady with the Lamp) drove herself on extensive rounds in a special cart pulled by a donkey she dubbed NHS – Ned's Hauling Service. She visited expectant mothers at Bunwell, delivered babies at Outwell, pills at Beachamwell, skin ointments at Wortwell and "all-clear" bulletins at Feltwell. On retirement she opened a bed-and-breakfast business at Bawdeswell.*

Fishing line – Sprat on a Hot Tin Roof

GREY POWER PARK

Granny Biffin, by a country mile Bronickle End's oldest and wisest indigenous remnant, sees no reason why more sanguine and supple senior citizens shouldn't be part of Norfolk's exciting drive for outdoor fun and fitness.

As a proud member of the Women's League of Health and Beauty, founded in 1930 by Mary Bagot Stack, she remains convinced renewable energy comes from within. "Too many people pushing 80 think that's enough exercise to be going on with. I don't know exactly how ancient I am but people assure me I don't look it."

This paragon of virtue when it comes to daring activities and fresh air recognises the county's good fortune in offering so many attractions to help meet a massive urge for an adrenalin rush prompted by too much bad television, supermarket shopping, speculative building, mobile phone prattling and tampering with the school curriculum.

"It's wonderful to get away from it all in places where you can snuggle up close to nature and look for fairies, magic dust, dinosaurs and the last coypu in Broadland. But it would be so much better if we golden oldies could go hunting for zip wires able to take our weight before joining another round of Pensioners' Paintball as dusk falls on Thetford Chase."

Granny Biffin, clearly determined to make a strong case in favour of Norfolk's first theme park for the elderly, even sanctioned a fact-finding visit to exotic distant climes by Abel Boddy, her close friend and fellow fitness enthusiast at the Bronickle End Saunatorium.

It is on the Isle of Wight that Codgerworld has been unveiled as Britain's only adventure playground created with "grey power and glory" in mind. Enthused by Abel's report and the chance of a few more hours of sunshine before October, Norfolk's most nimble nonagenarian is ready to scale new peaks in her campaign to convince the county that while growing old is mandatory, growing up is optional.

The Giant Tea Cup Ride has proved a stirring starter at Codgerworld with its challenge to get more tea in the mouth than in the saucer. The Dilatory Dodgems, nearly as popular, involves guiding mobility scooters around a pedestrianised track and avoiding potentially fatal crashes at speeds of up to two miles an hour.

There is a chilling-out area where over-excited geriatrics can relax in comfy chairs and enjoy re-runs of Countdown, Emmerdale, Escape to the Country and Who Do I Think I Am?

Abel Boddy stresses how queuing can be an issue on busy days. It takes a fair while for each visitor to clamber up The Giant Slide and the stair-lifts can't go any further. "Luckily, most pensioners think the queue itself is one of the rides. But for those who really don't have time to waste, there are special 'Eight years to live or fewer' queues."

He did suffer a fractured hip on The Aerial Runway but was delighted to find they sold replacements in the gift shop. "I still wish I hadn't accepted that free pint of bitter before trying my luck on The Tripletwist Trampoline."

There have been a few hiccups at Codgerworld to go with fluctuating blood pressures and hot flushes and so volunteers dressed like old-fashioned district nurses, complete with sit-up-and-beg-bicycles and baskets in front holding jars of frog spawn and digestive biscuits, are being drafted in for the peak summer season.

One unfortunate by-product of the theme park's success has been the reaction of some young people on the Isle of Wight. They have taken complaints about "threatening behaviour" of older folk to the local council and hinted they may leave their native island in search of less confrontational recreation in spots like Blackpool, Great Yarmouth, Holkham, Burnham Overy and Southend.

One teenager told Abel Boddy: "They take over the bus shelters, shout loudly at each other and even get on the bus without paying. Some passengers immediately stand up and hand over their seats because they're so afraid. You don't want that sort of thing in Norfolk, do you?"

While the Bronickle End think-tank must bear all possible repercussions in mind – and the occasional flare-up at Tuesday afternoon bingo organised by the local Silver Threads Club points to a growing appetite for aggravation in the parish – serious planning continues under the working title of Grey Power Park.

Brighter minds in the adjoining communities of Puckaterry Parva, Muckwash Magna and Little Coughwort are being encouraged to suggest possible names and locations for a new attraction likely to earn funding from the Arts Council, Norfolk Winners R Us, Holiday Here in November and the National Association for Those Still Hanging On in There.

Early title favourites include Confusercopse, despite its obvious echoes of Bewilderwood, Denturegitlorst, Extreme Snoozing, The Hereafter (so visitors can exclaim: "What am I here after?" without being asked to give an answer) and Hunt the Spectacles.

Meanwhile, Granny Biffin, exercising her right to totally ignore the passage of time and all those who treat it too seriously, looks forward to the media frenzy bound to accompany her latest big adventure.

"I'll tell 'em my age is a millinery secret" she mused. "I keep it under my hat."

Eastern Daily Press June 2013

There was a quack doctor from Dilham
Whose motto was "Cure 'em or kill 'em"
But his trade multiplied
For if anyone died
He'd play very fair and not bill 'em

CALL ME AN OLD BLUFFER - 6
WHAT DOES THE OLD WORD 'NUNTY' MEAN?

On slow side – This is an old exclamation directed at someone a bit slow in doing a job. Onlookers would cry "Nunty!" in mocking tones and offer instant advice as to how the task could be done quicker and better. It was used regularly at troshing time on the farm if anybody was slow, especially in feeding the drum. One of those useful words which could be employed as a verb or an adjective or simply as a plain Norfolk insult!

Plain speaking - The word simply means very plain and old-fashioned and was often used to describe Norfolk mawthers in country areas where the latest fashions were hardly likely to appear. The description applied to female dress only and may have been a rather clumsy form of something to do with the word "nun". In any event, those Norfolk gals were none too pleased to be labelled "nunty".

Eyes down -This is no more than a Norfolk corruption of ninety – you know, top of the house at bingo. In fact, it was often called out that way when lotto was played around our village halls. If the top number came out those filling in their cards would cry out "Nunty!" in chorus – and then laugh at their own plain silliness.

Going without – This is a clever old word used by women getting refreshments ready at cricket matches on the village scene. If a chap couldn't stop for tea because he had to nip back to the farm to help with milking or some other job, he was described as a "Nunty" – which meant, quite obviously, he wouldn't be there for tea!

Fishing line – A Star is Prawn

Sid Kipper, the modest multi-talented megastar
from St Just-near-Trunch.

Fishing line – The Cocklestall Heroes

WIT AND WISDOM OF SID KIPPER
A rare Norfolk word; Sheep

The reason we don't have many sheep in Norfolk now is we found out what caused them.

You see, years ago we had loads of sheep, due to what they called the Lowland Clearances. That was when the landlords got foreclosures, fenced off the land and threw all the peasants off it. Because they found that sheep kept the grass down just as well, plus you got the wool and the sheep didn't set fire to your hay ricks, or get with child by you and insist on maintenance. Well, a lamb don't take a lot of maintaining, anyhow.

So the landlords got rich, and built great churches to solve their consciences, and wondered why there was nobody left to go to them. And the proof is we've still got the churches, even though the sheep have moved on.

Round our way, there was another reason. The sheep were all kept on the Ups –near Northrups and Southrups –which is the high ground. So the breed was called Up Ewe. They were marvellous sheep. They gave fine wool, lovely meat, and they were always healthy.

The only trouble with them was they were very hard to sell. Well, you'd take an Up Ewe to market, and go up to the dealer and say, "Would you like to buy a sheep?" And he'd say,"What sort is it?" So you'd tell him.

And very often the sheep would escape in the ensuing fracas.

There was a young girl from Thorpe Marriott
Liked to drink, but she just couldn't carry it.
She'd quaff with a zest
Then whip off her vest
And kiss every Tom, Dick or Harriet.

Fishing line – Jurassic Carp

WHICH DRAMATIC FIGURE IS TELLING THE TRUTH?

Edmund Theodore Fisher – Yes, I am indeed a member of that most famous of theatrical families in local stage history – the Fishers. Throughout most of the 19th century we spelt glamour and romance in dozens of towns and scores of villages. My speciality was the Bard and I often reduced audiences to tears with my Othello, Hamlet Shylock and Richard lll. I was born in East Dereham and first made a dramatic mark as a pantomime fool with a group in the town called The Running Angels. Several other members of my family also took part. So that is me – the elegant, erect and mildly enigmatic Edmund Theodore Fisher – Theo to my intimates. My grave is in Dereham churchyard – my heavenly stage.

Rupert Mendoza – I set hearts a 'fluttering on stages in Norfolk and Suffolk in those wonderfully artistic years just before the first world war. I was born Rex Makepeace at Great Ryburgh, near Fakenham, the only child of Myrtle and Jem Makepeace. I adopted my theatrical name of Rupert Mendoza on auditioning for the part of a Spanish bullfighter in a now forgotten epic called Crimson Tear produced by the Swaffham Theatrical Company in 1899. The part propelled me to fame not only in East Anglia but also in London, York and Exeter. I concentrated on roles here in Norfolk after a nasty accident during a run at Drury Lane in London. I slipped off the stage and injuries left me unable to take any parts involving rapid movement. My speciality became Greek gods standing at the back of the stage glorying over both cast and audience.

Clifford J Arthurton – I was a famous actor with the Company of Comedians who performed in the Black Swan Playhouse just a few years before the first Norwich Theatre Royal was built and opened in 1758. As the name suggests, the Black Swan Playhouse – known inevitably as the Mucky Duck – was based in a famous old inn not far from St Peter Mancroft Church, and my father was landlord in the 1740s. I used my middle initial on all playhouse posters – but never revealed what it stood for. Some thought it was James, others Joshua – my father's name – but it really stood for Jacob, a name of which I was not fond in the slightest. Modesty ought to prevail here but it may help you if I confess that my Julius Caesar in Norwich, 1752, was ranked by many good critics as the finest interpretation ever seen in a British stage. "Toweringly effective" and "He has no peer" were just two of the plaudits. That's me, Clifford J Arthurton – and please keep quiet about the 'J'!

John Brunton – Tis I, forsooth, one of the most honoured names associated with the Norwich Theatre Royal. Whisper this name with reverence – John Brunton. It was during my management at the end of the 18th century that this splendid building must have reached the zenith of its fame. I was born in Norwich, son of a soap-boiler, and served my apprenticeship as a grocer in London before taking to the stage. Perhaps it was an apron stage in honour of my previous calling. I fathered three actress daughters of divine talent, Ann, Louie and Elizabeth, and we also had a son known as John Brunton Junior. He must be remembered in these parts as he opened the Lynn Theatre Royal so brilliantly in 1815. I am John Brunton Senior – a manager, an actor and a philanthropist who did his best in the names of religion and morality.

Festive fun in the air for another cracker of a show. Left to right - Sid Kipper, Keith Skipper, David Clayton, Canon Ivan Bailey and Roy Waller.

LATE ARRIVALS...
...FOR THE DIOCESAN BALL

My lords, ladies and gentlemen, please welcome our new incumbent at St Stephen's who can only stay a matter of weeks. Parson Through.

Please welcome now our good friends from the Convent of the Sacred Heart. The nun with the washing machine is Sistermatic and those carrying begging bowls and holding small radios to their ears are Little Transisters of the Poor.

And finally our curate Mark who's shortly off to Rome to play for the priests' football team made up of talented part-timers.... Interregnum!

NORFOLK FIRSTS: *Norfolk's first boy band, The Temperamental Seven, had their roots in Repps-with-Bastwick where they entertained at a local nightclub, The Pickled Onion, along with self-styled stripper, The Lady of Shallott. The band fell out over who should wear the coveted top hat as leader but were reunited 60 years later for a busking contest in Burnham Deepdale.*

Fishing line – Clam Every Mountain

ENGLISH AS SHE ARE SPOKE

I take it you already know
Of tough and bough and cough and dough?
Others may stumble but not you
On hiccough, thorough, lough and through?
Well done! And now you wish perhaps
To learn of less familiar traps?

Beware of heard, a dreadful word
That looks like beard and sounds like bird,
And dead: it's said like bed not bead –
For goodness sake don't call it deed!
Watch out for meat and great and threat
(They rhyme with suite and straight and debt).

A moth is not a moth in mother
Nor both in bother, broth in brother,
And here is not a match for there
Nor dear and fear for bear and pear,
And then there's dose and rose and lose
Just look them up – and goose and choose.

And cork and work and card and ward,
And font and front and word and sword,
And do and go and thwart and cart,
Come, come! I've hardly made a start!
A dreadful language? Man alive!
I'd mastered it when I was five!

NORFOLK FIRSTS: *Norfolk's first Apprentice Cobbler of the Year, sponsored by First Steps of Booton in 1949, was five-year-old Ivor Cutting from Edgefield. He went on to take do-it-yourself classes in Shelfanger, basket weaving in Stratton Strawless and hairdressing in Crimplesham.*

Fishing line – Kiss Me, Skate

WIT AND WISDOM OF SID KIPPER
The Trans-Norfolk Highway

The Trans-Norfolk Highway goes from Lynn to Mundesley, or vice-versa, depending on which way up you hold the map.

Mind you, some people say it don't exist. Well, they're just showing off their own ignorance, when they'd be far better hiding it under a bushel, because the road's even got a number. It's the B1145.

My antecedor, "Gentleman" Jack Kipper, had a famous ride along it, and he couldn't have done that if it weren't there, could he? No, he could not is the answer, in case you were wondering – or hidden under a bushel.

He was a notorious highwayman, because he rode a horse. If he'd been on foot he'd have been a footpad. The way to progress from one job to the other was by way of being a horse thief. On his ride, he notoriously leapt the turnpike bar at Gaywood Hall to avoid paying.

Unfortunately, his horse didn't, so old "Gent" had to pay to go back and get it; and then pay again to take it through. They were very strict in them days.

The Trans-Norfolk goes through loads of places. Places like North Elmham, which hundreds of years ago used to be a city, but got relegated after a run of poor results. And Reepham, which at one time had three churches, but one got razed not long after it got raised, in the Great Fire of Reepham in 1543. Another idea them Londoners nicked.

Then there's Cawston, which has its own whinery. And Aylsham, Banningham, Felmingham and North Walsham – in fact the Trans-Norfolk is full of hams, due to once being a major pig-droving route. Banningham is where they tried to stop it, but it was all to know of ale, as they say, and nothing come of it.

After Swafield, with its naturist reserve, and Knapton, which we don't talk about where I come from, at last it's Mundesley. And them four word's not something you hear said too often.

Of course, my little village of St Just-near-Trunch lies just off the Trans-Norfolk, so we get the breast of both worlds. We get the convenience of travel without all the hustle and bustle – although I don't know what people have got against bustles anyway.

CALL ME AN OLD BLUFFER - 8
WHAT ON EARTH WAS "CROTCH – TROLLING"?

Nurse Troller – Crotch-trolling was the charming name given to youngsters' antics as they waited for the nit nurse at the village school. It is believed to have been first used at Baconsthorpe in the mid-1880s when a notorious nurse called Edith Troller did the rounds with Dettol and such to get rid of head lice. As the word implies, itching and scratching were not confined to the scalp and so nurses were asked for remedies to treat all parts of the anatomy.

Take a break – Crotch-trolling was a form of knitting employed by East Anglian women taking a break from work on the land, especially at potato-picking time. It could be done in formation with three or more participants taking it in turn to use the needles and then pass them on. There were crotch-trolling championships at the end of the 19th century at Wolferton on the Royal Estate when the Prince of Wales provided a trophy for the winners.

Poachers' delight – Crotch-trolling was an old method of angling for pike used extensively on the Norfolk Broads. Fishermen had no rod but had the usual reel and with the help of a crotch stick they could hurl bait a considerable distance into the water and then draw it gently towards them. It was much used by poachers as there was no rod or pole to betray their dark intentions. It looked as if they were simply passing the time away.

Musical cheers – Crotch-trolling was an early form of improvisation on piano or organ – and one famous exponent, Jacob Large of Kirby Bedon, used it to stirring effect on a harmonium he played in the village chapel. He claimed to offer two tunes at once in the event of some members of the congregation switching from one to the other during a hymn with more than a single format. Jacob could also add a clinking noise on his instrument if the collection was being taken at the same time.

Fishing line – Salmon Chanting Evening

Likely lads Sid and Skip plot a bit more mischief with a Norfolk flavour.

Fishing line - Mackerel and Mabel

HORSE PLAY

Every Tuesday at King's Lynn Cattle Market a chicken farmer would arrive with a few poults to sell. He had a notorious reputation for beating his horse unmercifully.

He would sell his poults, and then make his way to a nearby pub where he drank his profits away. He then returned to his horse and cart, whipping his horse harshly, and would make his way to his small-holding just outside King's Lynn.

Invariably the man would be seen asleep on his cart with his faithful horse making its own way to his home.

One day young farmers decided to give the man a lesson he would not forget.

The following Tuesday they followed the farmer into the pub and proceeded to get him thoroughly drunk. Once they had succeeded they lifted the man into his cart and drove it to his home.

On arrival they carried him into his grubby parlour and placed him in his chair in front of the fireplace.

They then removed the horse from the shafts, fed and watered it well. They then took the cart to pieces, re-assembled it in the parlour, and placed the horse back in its shafts, tying the horse to a weight so that it stood facing him when he awoke!

The farmers said they never saw the man beat his horse again!

Rev. Ivan Lilley

There was an old feller from Costessey
Whose wife was unbearably bostessey
So he taped up her mouth
East to west, north to south
Then he cried "that'll shut you up Flostessey!"

Fishing line – Last Night on the Back Perch

NORFOLK FIRSTS: *Norfolk's first licensed fortune teller, "Lucky" Heather Borrow, set up her Open Palms headquarters at Reedham in the early 1900s. As she dealt exclusively in favourable forecasts her waiting room was always packed. She lost all her savings through gambling on Hoe and Oby becoming Norfolk's first overspill communities.*

Fishing line – Don't Koi For Me, Argentuna

POPPYLAND PROBING

Lips of fire-engine red loitered around teeth of drifting-snow white. She crossed her legs with enough slow sensuality to evoke fond memories for a legion of winter-gnarled veterans queuing for 'flu jabs on a mufflers-and-mittens morning.

Her fur stole threatened to spring alive, desert those elegant shoulders and cause trouble for my mug of tea steaming in a world of its own by a brand new desk calendar and a shabby old copy of The A-Z of Sidestrand Speakeasys.

It was too late to give my top-floor garret of an office a veneer of class. So I relaxed, persuaded my wobbly chair to stop scraping the bare floor and offered her a cigarette from a new case I'd bought on the last case solved.

A broken halo of smoke sat over our silence. Suddenly she snapped open a shiny crimson handbag, fussed inside like a mole packing hastily for a holiday and lifted out a small black-and-white photograph into the light.

She fixed me with the sort of doleful look my secretary Velda reserved for pleas to increase her wages before she walked out in a huff to marry a rich attorney from LA.

That's Lower Aylsham.

"How can Poppyland Pimpernels Investigation Agency help you, Miss..... or is it Mrs......?" My initial inquiry fell on a plump cushion of warm breaths and earnest smiles.

"Just call me Ladybird. That's my stage name. Real-life details to follow if you take the job and I agree to your terms." She purred like a kitten needing a fondle before a basket nap. I fought to keep pet habits to myself, habits I'd overcooked to my detriment on that Thanksgiving pilgrimage to LA.

That's Langham Airfield.

Haggling lasted for nearly 30 seconds of quality time at the start of a brand new year of fearless probing, prescribing and procrastinating. I needed the work badly after tasting the acrid smoke of the defeated all too often.

I had to keep on feeding the fire of ambition, albeit in a more homely grate since stepping way out of my class and beyond my patch in a vain search for the Matlaske Falcon.

Fishing line – Prawn to be Wild

Ladybird's photograph introduced me to her missing beau, a real estate agent called Edge whose last known address was the optimistically-labelled Sunrise Boulevard on Happisburgh Cliffs.

He specialised in mansions with wedding-cake decorations around double dormer windows and a Rolls Royce Silver Wraith or Chrysler Sedan living outside. A man of simple tastes. Simply luxurious.

Cometh the hour, cometh the boy – time to engage the burgeoning talents of my latest bloodhound with acne, work experience wonder Desmond, on loan to me from the scholarly confines of LA.

That's Litcham Academy.

Still a few rough edges to smooth out before Desmond can frame a few detection diplomas and so cover damp patches near the office door. I just know he will refer to our new client as "that bishy-barney-bee mawther."

An air of rustic innocence can open doors hitherto locked to more genteel inquiries but my silver-tongued sidekick must accept that not all members of society enjoy being hailed as "my ole bewty."

I served my angst-ridden apprenticeship with Cromer Crime Crackers back in a golden age before second homers, bobble-hatted twitchers and celebrity chefs rendered it all but impossible to know where the next suspect was coming from.

Sherlock Holmes, Father Brown, Gideon of the Yard, Charlie Chan, Philip Marlowe – all useful role models as I scanned a bank holiday beach full of occupied hand-knitted one-piece costumes to find The Smooth Villain who put Itching Powder in the Mixed Bathing Machines.

If that was my finest hour, The Case of the Shrinking Gansey had to be clocked in as a close second. I blush even now at discovering why the fisherman's jersey failed to cover his modesty after so many drip-dry excursions into the old German Ocean.

With such stirring exploits and a stiff breeze behind me, I unleashed Poppyland Pimpernels Investigation Agency on an ill-prepared world following an internationally-recognised course marked LA.

That's Lakenheath Associates.

While the menu may be different, and clients no longer throw me incredulous glances when I include a good square meal every day and a new tuxedo when necessary on a list of expenses, a private eye's

Fishing line – Bream Lover (Bobby Darin)

sup with mystery and intrigue in North Norfolk remains tantalisingly tasty.

Ladybird has flown. She'll be back to reopen those dainty wings of supplication on my humble runway of hope. Desmond is out on his BSA Bantam looking for Mr Edge.

A new year has dawned. We must be worthy of its creation and its challenges. I'm heading for LA.

That's Lazy Afternoon.

Eastern Daily Press, January, 2010

A Norfolk driver seeking the right way to summer

Fishing line – Zing Went the Strings of my Carp

CALL ME AN OLD BLUFFER - 9
WHICH IS THE REAL RUSTIC RITUAL?

Tight Garter Day – At West Winton in North Yorkshire on Easter Monday, it is still customary to celebrate Tight Garter Day, a rustic ritual dating back to the Middle Ages. A dozen unmarried men under 30 form an orderly line on the village green. They are dressed in "bucolic attire" of smock, felt hat and loose-fitting pantaloons. Selected unwed maidens then step forward to place garters around the left leg of their chosen swain and pull it tight to the point of it becoming painful ... an indication of close attachment to come. Should any couple get married after this ritual, the parish has to provide a reward of 50 guineas and a free wedding reception.

Punky Night – This is celebrated in and around Hinton St George, near Yeovil in Somerset, in the last week of October. A punky is a lantern made from a hollowed out mangel-wurzel. It contains a candle whose light shines through a design etched in the outer skin. On the last Thursday night in October, children carry these round the village boundary and through the streets collecting money and chanting:
It's Punky Night tonight, it's Punky Night tonight
Give us a candle, give us a light
It's Punky Night tonight!
Later comes the crowning of the Punky King and Queen, children who have collected most for charity.

Barley on Calf – The old harvest ritual of carrying the last sheaf of barley on the back of a suckling calf through the village street when all is safely gathered in is still celebrated in Great Wishford, near Salisbury. The calf is then offered a drink of freshly-brewed ale at the local pub, The Merry Monk. The sheaf of barley, fresh beer and a young animal are combined symbols of rural creation and fertility. The whole event is completed as the pub landlord chants:

> Barley to brew, barley to brew,
> Come inside and sup a few
> Barley or calf, barley or calf
> Harvest Home deserves a half.

Cough-Drop Corner – At Titchborne in Hampshire, they still mark Good Friday with an old ceremony called Cough-Drop Corner. It goes back to the 16th century when parish records show it was first enacted in the most northerly part of the churchyard after a virulent outbreak of the coughing epidemic which it was claimed had taken six lives. The parson, the Rev Septimus Hyde, and his three churchwardens decided to "helpe clear Mother Earthe's throate" with an anti-coughing potion or tablet dropped in the ground on the holiest day of the year. In more modern times, cough mixture or cough drops have been deemed suitable for the occasion. It is thought Titchborne is the only place to conduct such a ceremony.

NORFOLK FIRSTS: *Norfolk's first serious attempt to integrate rich newcomers and second-homers with hardened locals unfolded on Sheringham beach in 1909. Celebrity suffragettes, aspiring actresses and trainee bankers were invited to spend weekends under canvas with samphire pickers, cockle gatherers and crab fishermen. The experiment ended when women got the vote and cockle quotas were imposed by Germany.*

Fishing line – Caviarederci Roma

LATE ARRIVALS...
...FOR THE LOCAL PRESS BALL

Mr Editor-in-chief, ladies and gentlemen of the press, please welcome Mr Horry Krishna, newly-appointed correspondent for the Eastern Delhi Press. He's had a Punjab – but it doesn't work.

Your appreciation, please, for Mr Puff Pastry, ready to take up a fresh role filling in for son Flaky as baking expert on the Eastern Doyley Press. Mr Pastry, bred and born in Norwich, says he wasn't really cut out for the job – but it earns an honest crust.

Now would you please welcome a special guest from the capital, Gizza Fagg, chain-smoking features editor of the Sunday Sensation. He's very sorry – but he can't stop hacking.

My lords, ladies and gentlemen, please extend a hearty welcome to Mr Clarke Kent, skydiving correspondent for the Beccles and Bunjee Journal.

And finally on this most auspicious occasion, please welcome the celebrated correspondent for Burnham Thorpe, Mr Horry Nelson ....
soon to have his own column.

A granny who comes from Pott Row
Went out to a Chippendales' show
Though she got home alright
Grandad soon had a fright
When her pacemaker started to glow

A Sunday School teacher from Caister
Was shocked when a bounder unlaced her
She cried "I am chaste"
Which was just to his taste
So when she ran home then he chased her

Fishing line – Not The Nine o'Clock Newts

WIT AND WISDOM OF SID KIPPER
Old Norfolk custom; ploughing

Years ago, people used to sing about the painful plough, although I reckon that just mean they were doing it all wrong.

But there's nothing new about that, I mean, they reckon that even more years ago they used to plough with oxen. Well, that must have been a sight is all I can say. Imagine a horse pulling an ox up and down a field, hoping to turn the sod over. That would be pointless, anyhow, because whichever side of the sod you used, it would still be an ox.

The modern plough started because of an accident in Suffolk in 1803, though it pains me to say so. Howsomever, the bloke the accident happened to was a Norfolk boy, Robert Ransome, from Wells-on-Sea (as it was then called). He found his accidental plough share would stay sharp, while an ox would always go blunt.

When he'd worked out how to make the accident deliberate he became a champion plough maker. Eventually he also went into lawn mowers, but that's extremely dangerous, so don't try it at home. Try it close to an Accident and Emergency Department.

The custom bit is because of plough matches, which were held in the autumn – well, they still are in some parts. What happened was everyone met up on a particular Sunday, all with their ploughs, and if you could find two ploughs the same you won a goldfish.

Some places couldn't afford ploughs, so they often had cheese pairing instead. They chose a Sunday because in those days you couldn't get a drink unless you were a traveller, so they all travelled to each other's pubs and got pickled as lilies.

Another custom they did was Oxo, which was a sort of bingo using redundant oxen.

Fishing line – A Midsummer Night's Bream

In some parts they had a problem with illegal ploughing. In order to get a better price for their crops, people would sneak out at night and plough in someone else's.

Obviously, the someone else would be on the lookout for it and very often the illegal ploughers would be disturbed – unless you think they must have been disturbed in the first place to do what they were doing, in which case I suppose you'd have to say they were even more disturbed. If that happened the illegal ploughers would run off in all directions.

And if you reckon I'm making all this up, just remember the song about it – *We Plough the Fields and Scatter.*

NORFOLK FIRSTS: *Norfolk's most eccentric cricket club scorer was "Googly" Harcourt, who did the honours for Stow Bardolph Stumpers in the late 1890s. He used a quill pen and dressed in the costume designed for French cricket at his private school in Bale. He spoke five foreign languages including Broad Norfolk.*

Fishing line – Roe, Roe, Roe the Boat

CALL ME AN OLD BLUFFER - 10
WHO IS THE GENUINE COASTAL ENTERTAINER?

Sheik Ben Ali – I am a true Bengali magician with a famous catchphrase: "Nothing inside, nothing outside!" Some may even recall how in 1936 I produced and appeared in an all-Indian show at Great Yarmouth before taking that revue all round the world. Perhaps I'm most fondly remembered as a solo act featuring many amazing tricks with coins. Some say I should have worked for the International Monetary Fund. My catchphrase "Nothing inside, nothing outside!" came from one of those tricks with an empty paper bag. I also stunned audiences with my Ali Baba speciality as I mass produced bodies from a row of sealed jars.

Rustic Ronnie – Yes, I am that loveable comedian with just a whiff of true country pedigree. A Norfolk jacket and shiny buskins set me apart as a man of real taste upon the stage. But my local yokel humour did upset one or two council worthies around the seaside holiday camps and theatres. My catchphrase, "Well, I'll be spanked with a ferret's tail on a wet Wednesday morning!" drew sharp criticism from a certain mayor of Yarmouth in 1952. We'll keep his name out of it to avoid embarrassment – but after he made headlines in the local paper we had full houses every night throughout the summer. Serve him right for sticking his nose in where it wasn't wanted! He should have known better than to tangle with Rustic Ronnie.

The Great Jimnastico – Yes, that's right, the Great Jimnastico. I rippled my superbly developed muscles to set female hearts a 'fluttering back in the late 1940s and early 1950s. My strongman act took in several summer shows along the east coast although my favourite was always the Sandcastle Theatre at Mablethorpe, my home town in Lincolnshire. For many the highlight of my turn dressed like Tarzan was to swing from one side of the stage to the other on a rope, uttering blood-curdling cries and carrying three bathing beauties under each arm. I'm proud to say I never dropped one in eight years at the top of my profession.

Fishing line – In Your Oyster Bonnet

Sweet Nellie Duncan – I spent many seasons in seaside theatres up and down the country, including appearances at Yarmouth, Gorleston and Cromer. I did a couple of one-night variety shows in Hunstanton – but way down the bill with my mixture of light opera and tricks with strategically placed balloons. Just when it seemed my act might be totally serious, I would change direction, blow up the balloons, always yellow and red, and introduce a bit of knockabout fun. "Nellie Duncan – but not disorderly!" was my motto. My nephew, Johnny, found fame as a singer. You can probably remember Johnny Duncan and the Blue Grass Boys with Last Train to San Fernando.

Lady in waiting .... Carol Bundock gathers her thoughts in the dressing-room before another cheerful outing on stage with Should The Team Think?

Fishing line – Anchovies Aweigh!

This is how a certain member of the Should The Team Think? panel asked to be billed for a show when self-esteem teetered on the brink of extinction:

Willowy, enigmatic, adventurous with a rare taste for travel. Has been to Swaffham twice when it wasn't Market Day.

Very good to his wife. Only goes home on Wednesdays. Still carries matinee idol looks. He did one matinee at Norwich Theatre Royal – and has been idle ever since.

Harbours ambition to be shot dead by a jealous husband when he's 94. Once wrote to Lonely Hearts Club in Sheringham. They wrote back and said they weren't that lonely.

Reached last 32 in the Cromer and District Heat of "Nelson's County Hev Got Talent" but his party piece did not impress the judges. He did the splits over a Bunsen burner singing I Who Have Nothing. And for an encore presented a Norfolk version of Great Balls of Fire!

Finished up with an audition for Singe Something Simple.

A self-made man who worships his creator.

*****

This same panellist was asked for a selection of stories he would most like to write or read in the *Eastern Daily Press*. Here are his suggestions;

Transport Minister gives go-ahead for singling of A11, cobbling of A47 and removal altogether of A140.

Prospective MPs must live in area they want to represent for five years before seeking Westminster seats.

Incinerator catches fire at County Hall.

Single currency for Norfolk agreed in Brussels.

IMF moves to Ten Mile Bank. Winfarthing decimalised.

Quidenham worth thirty bob.

Norfolk Independence Party makes big inroads in local and national elections.

AFTERWORD

This letter sent to David Clayton at Radio Norfolk after a Should The Team Think? recording at a rural village hall underlines the deep affection in which the programme has been held over the years. It also reveals the depth of genuine local humour:

Dear Mr Clayton,

Surely the BBC can find better things to do with its money and time than subsidise four half-wits on a public platform with nothing useful to say in front of people who ought to be at home doing something better in the privacy of their own boudoirs.

People simply don't have sensible hobbies any more. We had to make our own amusement, even on the rough council estate where I was brought up. I remember the rag-and-bone man pulling up in 1936 for a pint of shandy at our local pub. When he came out his horse was on bricks.

That's the sort of inventive thinking this country needs to get going again. I am a regular Radio Norfolk listener but I think you have now reached the lowest ebb in the thirty odd years you have been trying to enlighten us.

When I said half-wit I may have been exaggerating. Make that a quarter between them – and then I think I may be veering towards the generous.

Yours sincerely,

Disgusted Listener from Litcham.

PS – The panel may be interested to know – if they can concentrate for more than a second – that the first time I went ski-ing I wasn't very good at it and broke a leg. Thank goodness it wasn't one of mine. Keep up the good work and I look forward to hearing the recording of this evening's inane ramblings at a later date when I am at a loss for something constructive to do.

It'll never replace Dick Barton

A 1950 potato harvest in full swing as Norfolk relishes its agricultural roots.

A SORT OF NORFOLK DICTIONARY

[It may help to say some words out loud
if a new dawn is slow in breaking]

abdicate: give up all hope of having a flat stomach

absentee: missing golf peg

accolade: drink for good children

aconite: special show for Mr Bilk

aftermath: relaxing at end of algebra class

ambrosia: inability to remember last time you had creamed rice

Angular: as opposed to BBC regional television

aperitif: two dentures. If both in middle, that's central eating

archives: where Noah kept his bees

aromatic: autopilot for archers

arsenic: result of sitting on sharp instrument

artery: study of paintings

astute: bit like a weasel

balderdash: rapidly receding hairline

baloney: where some hemlines fall

barbecue: waiting for a haircut

bare: alcoholic beverage usually served in pints or half-pints

barium: what doctors do when patients pass on

benign: what all eight-year-olds hanker for

betterannerhebbin: much improved, thanks

bide: past tense of buy

bidet: nothing like D-Day

blunderbuss: vehicle used to smuggle pregnant girls out of the village

boomerang: to jeer at a pudding. (say out loud)

Fishing line – Oh, What a Beautiful Marlin

brunette: type of tea strainer

buckshee: confused rabbit

bungalow: word first used in Norfolk when a builder told one of his workers "Bung a low roof on that one and that'll be different."

cardiology: study of knitwear

carnation: country where everyone drives

caterpillar: scratching post for cats

caustic: used to beat off crows

champagne: pretend injury

chipmonk: deeply religious squirrel

claustrophobia: allergic to Father Christmas

coffee: person upon whom one coughs

cohabit: pigeon impressionist

comeback: half a boomerang

commotion: as in Holy Commotion at the parish church

concubine: as in concubine harvester

contour: disappointing trip

contradictive: as in contradictive pills

copulate: admonishment for tardy policeman

corfu: Norfolk angler's response to questions about his progress

coronation: as in Coronation milk

counterfeit: "I've got two!" she says

cuckoo: chocolate bedtime drink

curfew: a doctor's minimum aim

cutlass: tipsy girl

"Take it easy, old partner"

decanter: to slow down a horse

dependable: excellent swimmer

diagnostic: Welsh non-believer

dilate: to live longer

Dick Turnip: Norfolk's first dyslexic highwayman. He rode Bleck Bass

disparaging: being rude about a south Norfolk town

diverse: Welsh poetry

Dunham: Great and Little, last villages to be named in Norfolk – "Thass Dunham!"

effluent: stinking rich

electrocution: as in electrocution lessons for newcomers to Norfolk

Fishing line – Crab Caught a Train at King's Crustacean

emulsion: as in breaking down when overcome with emulsion

esplanade: to attempt an explanation while drunk

evacuated: as in evacuated milk

fibula: a small lie

flabbergasted: appalled at discovering how much weight one has gained

flagrant: tramp with a whip

flatulence: emergency vehicle used to pick up someone run over by a steamroller

fortification: two twentifications

frisbeetarianism: belief that after death the soul flies up to the roof and gets stuck there

futility: as in futility rites, common in Norfolk

gargoyle: olive-flavoured mouthwash

gladiator: satisfied cannibal

gloamin': as in gloamin' warbling, often heard on Cley Marshes at dusk

goad: past tense of go

gobbledegeek: one who studies official documents

goblet: small turkey

goodwill: one in which everything is bequeathed to me!

gruesome: gardening boast

gullible: easily impressed by birds

guzunder: chamber pot

hangover: wrath of grapes

hiccup: drinking vessel for country yokels

highfalutin': as in footballer Ron Davies used to jump high for Luton

homer: plenty of seconds in Norfolk

hootenanny: horn fixed to pram by precocious infant

hostile: as on stable roof

humdinger: honeycart with a bell

hurricane: Abel's call to his slouching brother

icing: even if I don't know the tune

idealise: ones that can see properly

impotent: distinguished, well known

impregnable: unable to have children (same as inconceivable)

inbred: born in a pub

inkling: often result of pen-top emotions

intense: scouting jamboree

jargon: Norfolk exercise before breakfast

jockstrap: handy for passengers standing on Scottish trains

ketchup: source of latest news

keptathometogoataterin': excuse in note from Norfolk mother whose boy had been absent from school for several days

khaki: some drivers have to hunt for it

kibbutz: were made for walking

legend: your foot

libido: swimming pool for broad-minded

lingerie: loitering in underwear department

logarithm: lumberjack dance

Fishing line – Mackerel the Knife

lunatic: for getting sums right on the moon

lympth: to walk with a lisp

malady: it often lingers on

manifestation: railway halt for ghosts

manuscript: written for many years by Sir Alex Ferguson

maritime: wedding day

mayhem: slightly lower than in April

menopause: give women a chance to speak

metronome: underground railway for little people

midriff: highlight of guitar solo

misanthrope: she dislikes people (Miss Ann Thrope)

misgivings: many a man has awoken with her!

morbid: higher offer

McSpreader: leading Norfolk clan

naive: Adam certainly was!

napkin: sleepy relatives

negligent: absentmindedly answering the door wearing only a night dress

networking: local fishermen get together on beach

nitworking: old-fashioned school nurse on her rounds

nickname: goes with your prison number

nitrates: cheaper than day rates

nostrum: guitar without strings

Fishing line – You Don't Send Me Flounders Anymore

Sheringham fishermen networking

oblique: rough Irish weather

octopus: cat with eight legs

offspring: prefers autumn

Old Year's Night: New Year's Eve

otherwise: Ernie's brother

outpatient: person who has fainted

overcast: play with too many characters

overrate: cricket umpires' responsibility

pantomime: underwear for hard of hearing

paradox: two physicians

paraffin: as in I love Paraffin the springtime

parsnip: Norfolk vasectomy

Fishing line – I Never Smelt This Way Before

parasite: Eiffel Tower is on one

patisserie: Irish baker

penshuner: retired writer

penultimate: best possible writing tool

pewter: tankard – but also Norfolk shorthand for a very clever machine

pharmacist: helper on the land

physiology: study of effervescent drinks

pillory: Norfolk chemist shop

polarise: some bears have them

polyanthus: replies from parrot with a lisp

porcupine: missing the old pig

portrait: unpleasant characteristic

promiscuous: shameless on seafront

propagate: for a proper field

propaganda: for a proper goose

protectorate: wages for a bodyguard

Pullet Surprise: Norfolk literary award for best cookery book of the year

queue: usually pronounced "kew" in Norfolk

quiche: usually pronounced "quicky" in Norfolk Take care how you ask for one.

quick: noise made by dyslexic duck

quire: very tuneful on paper

quoit: as in "I feel quoit good today"

raconteur: common misrepresentation of "wreckonteur", someone who talks about marine salvaging adventures

rampage: violent sheep

rampart: could be good for ewe!

ratchet: bit bigger than a mouse dropping

reindeer: weather prognosis as in " That look like rain dear."

relief: what many trees do in spring

reverie: strange dreams about vicars

ricochet: Irish full-back

rudimentary: rough sort of school

rubberneck: one way of relaxing the wife

satellite: it happens to bonfires. Used to be haystacks when workers got ratty

satire: extra cushion

scintillate: some people do, but others turn in early

secret: something you tell one person at a time

sediment: as in "Thass what he said he meant."

seizure: Roman emperor

semi-skilled: as in a pint of semi-skilled milk

senile: best go to Egypt for that

shamrock: not as hard as the real stuff

simpleton: easy century for a top batsman

sitcom: new website for armchair browsers

somersault: nearly as good as winter pepper

soupcon: cry from the kitchen – "Soup's on!"

specific: ocean nowhere near Norfolk

stalemate: leading cause of divorce

suburbia: where they tear out trees and flowers and then name streets after them

succeed: toothless budgies have to

suffocate: bit like Norfolkate

suggestive: popular brand of biscuits

Fishing line – Crabaret

symmetry: no, not a Norfolk burial place – it's the art of not boiling over

syntax: very few pay this tariff on immorality

tarmac: expression of gratitude towards Scotsman

toothache: pain that drives one to extraction

truant: as opposed to a false one

truculent: bad-tempered lorry driver

tunic: or not to nick – the burglar's dilemma

underlying: telling fibs in a tunnel

undertaker: potholing guide

unicorn: student humour

USA: Other Side of Attleborough

unwary: not tired

velocipede: getting drunk quickly

verdigris: constant interrogation to extract information

vice-versa: rude poet

viligante: Norfolk corruption of vigilante to denote someone who moves into the parish and opposes everything

violin: dirty pub

warehouse: someone who turns into a house at the full moon

wassanwotterwuz: declining health

wossitgotterdewwiyew?: gentle Norfolk inquiry

wisteria: excitement over local garden show

x-ray: former fish

yule: as in "Yule get wrong if yew dunt hurry up."

zakkly: Norfolk way to finish exactly right!

Land army drill in Norfolk, 1950s-style

Fishing line – Must stop – and break the halibut of a lifetime!

Call Me An Old Bluffer

Answers

1. **SPOT REAL LOCAL REMEDY** (p14)	Cowpat capers
2. **REAL MEANING OF 'LAGARAG'** (p23)	Lazy streak
3. **REAL CHRISTMAS CUSTOM** (p27)	Maidens' watch
4. **REAL MEANING OF 'DAFTER'** (p32)	Girl talk
5. **WHICH ONE FELL FOUL OF LAW?** (p38)	Arsenic and dumplings
6. **WHAT DOES 'NUNTY' MEAN?** (p43)	Plain speaking
7. **DRAMATIC FIGURE TELLING TRUTH** (p46)	John Brunton
8. **WHAT WAS 'CROTCH – TROLLING'?** (p52)	Poachers' delight
9. **REAL RUSTIC RITUAL** (p59)	Punky Night
10. **GENUINE COASTAL ENTERTAINER** (p64)	Sheik Ben Ali

An Ingoldisthorpe widow, though squireless
In sleeping with men was quite tireless
She treated each session
With utmost discretion
Now it's all been exposed on the wireless!